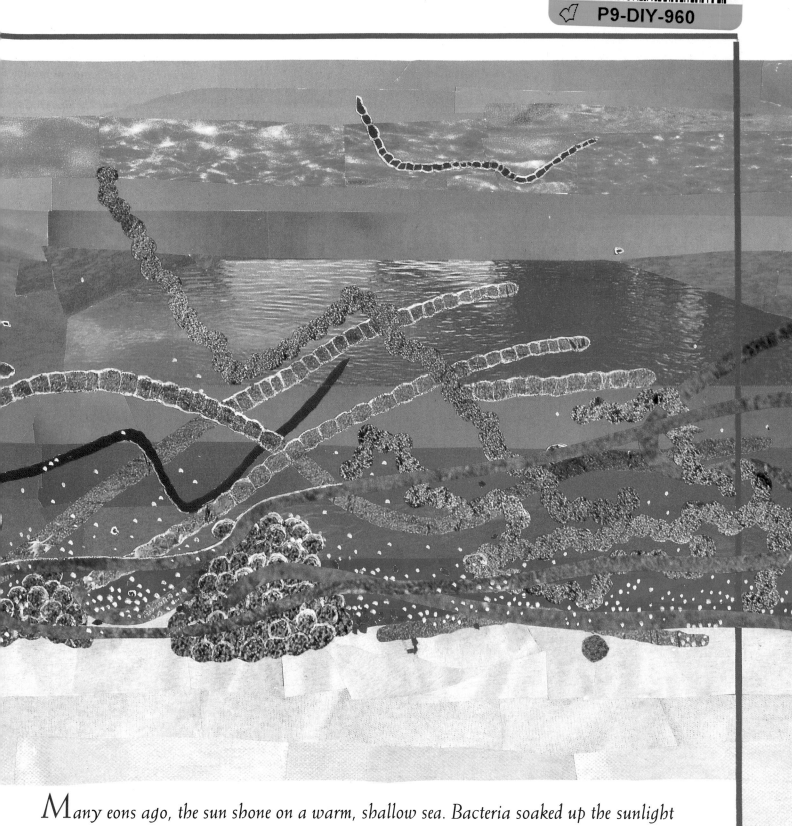

Many eons ago, the sun shone on a warm, shallow sea. Bacteria soaked up the sunlight and multiplied, building around themselves thin, sticky mats like giant lily pads. The mats caught floating particles until they got too thick for sunlight to get through; the bacteria glided and grew up to the surface and built again. Over millions of years, the mats were compressed into limestone layers hundreds of feet deep and hundreds of miles wide.

Volcanoes erupted to the north, sending clouds of ash onto the sea. The sea dried up, and the seabed became swampland for millions of years. Then the sea returned, killing the swamp plants. Beside the sea, mountains were pushed up; mud and sand drained off to cover everything and pressed the dead swamp plants into coal. Eventually the layers of sandstone, limestone, ash, and coal began to crinkle. They folded, twisted, and turned upside down.

These molded layers of earth are the southern Appalachian Mountains.

Rain fell on the mountains as they formed. Trees sprouted and covered the land with forests, sheltering wildlife. Rain seeped through the soil into the limestone. Drop by drop the water ate out underground caverns; the drops ran together and flowed into the light again as pale green creeks, which coursed down the mountainsides to join the great, winding Tennessee River.

Copyright © 1996 by Molly Bang

All rights reserved. No part of this publication may be reproduced or transmitted in any form or by any means, electronic or mechanical, including photocopy, recording, or any information storage and retrieval system, without permission in writing from the publisher.

Requests for permission to make copies of any part of the work should be mailed to: Permissions Department, Harcourt Brace & Company, 6277 Sea Harbor Drive, Orlando, Florida 32887-6777.

Gulliver Green is a registered trademark of Harcourt Brace & Company.

LC 94-44776

ISBN 0-15-216345-X

The text type was set in Weiss.
The display type was set in Bernhard Antique.
This book was printed with soya-based inks on Leykam recycled paper, which contains more than 20 percent postconsumer waste and has a total recycled content of at least 50 percent.
Production supervision by Warren Wallerstein and Pascha Gerlinger
Designed by Linda Lockowitz

First edition

A B C D E

Gulliver Green® Books focus on various aspects of ecology and the environment, and a portion of the proceeds from the sale of these books will be donated to protect, preserve, and restore native forests.

This Tennessee River Valley and these Appalachian Mountains, with their rippling, gurgling, pale green creeks, were like a little heaven on earth.

The people who lived there named one of the creeks the Chattanooga.

ABOUT 200 YEARS AGO, new settlers came from across the Appalachians and built factories along the banks of Chattanooga Creek. More people moved in, until a city grew up there. The people built still more factories, and everyone emptied their factory wastes into the water.

The creek bed became thick, black, stinking, tarry sludge.

Recently, scientists took samples of the sludge. They found that it contained large amounts of thirty-three poisons, and they declared the creek "the most polluted waterway in the southeastern United States."

What could people who lived near the creek do now? Even if all the factories cleaned up their wastes, toxins from the creek bed would still seep up into the water. Could the city dredge up the sludge and clean it?

Burning the sludge would cost WAY too much, and besides, the smoke and ashes might still be full of toxins. Trucking it away and burying it would only move the poisons to another place.

Nobody knew what to do.

2,4-dimethylphenol

naphthalene

benzo(a)anthracene

benzo(ghi)perylene

1,2,4-trichlorobenzene

fluoranthene

benzo(a)pyrene

alpha-BHC

aldrin

1,4-dichlorobenzene

acenaphthene

benzylbutylphthalate

anthracene

indeno(1,2,3-cd)pyrene

dibenzo(a,h)anthracene

bis(2ethylhexyl)phthalate

One day a member of the Chattanooga City Council read about a man from Massachusetts who had a peculiar idea about sewage. He said that our sewage is not a waste to get rid of but a precious resource we should save and use with care.

This man built greenhouses and filled them with tanks. He filled the tanks with tropical plants and marsh plants and flowering plants and vegetables and trees—and fish and snails. Then he fed the plants on sewage water. Gray, disgusting water went in one end of a greenhouse, fed the plants, and poured out pure and clean on the other side. The man called his greenhouses Living Machines because living plants and creatures did all the work of cleaning the water.

The city councilman wondered if these Living Machines could clean up toxic sludge as well as they cleaned up sewage water. He and the other council members invited the man down to look at Chattanooga Creek.

YUCK!

THIS IS ECOLOGICAL ENGINEERING!

The man and the council members walked along the banks of the creek. They saw houses empty and boarded up because nobody wanted to live there. Those who did live there told of children always getting sick and people dying too young.

The group came to a big dump on the creek bank. Across the creek they saw a school yard where children were playing on the slope just a couple of feet from the water.

The man watched the children for a while and said, "So far my Living Machines have only cleaned normal sewage *water*. This is thick sludge, and it is full of poisons we don't know how to clean up yet. It might be impossible to do.

"But I want to try. If you give me some of the sludge, I'll make a small Living Machine and do an experiment with it, and we'll see what happens."

Several weeks later, workers waded out into the creek and hammered long, hollow pipes into the sludge until they hit solid rock—about four feet down. When they pulled the pipes out, sludge was stuck inside. The workers drained it into a large bottle.

Most of the officials watching this operation were sure the work was useless. Some of the poisons had been in the mud for over 150 years, and most of the new ones would not break down for thousands of years if they were left alone. How could a greenhouse full of plants clean up this mess?

But the man wasn't discouraged. He was planning his experimental machine.

He decided to make it with two different tanks. The small tank would hold the toxic sludge. The big tank would be an aquarium. He would exchange small amounts of water between them.

THOSE IGNORANT HUMANS! THEY MAKE STUFF SO TOXIC THEY HAVE TO WEAR **MOON SUITS** TO SAMPLE IT!

BUT THEY LET THEIR **CHILDREN** PLAY IN THE SAME WATER!

WHAT DID THEY THINK WOULD HAPPEN TO **US**?

THEY DIDN'T THINK!

At the end of his experiment, the government would do two tests: one on the water and one on the sludge. If both the sludge and the water were clean, this would prove that Living Machines could clean the poisonous sludge.

But how did he expect the toxins to just *disappear*?

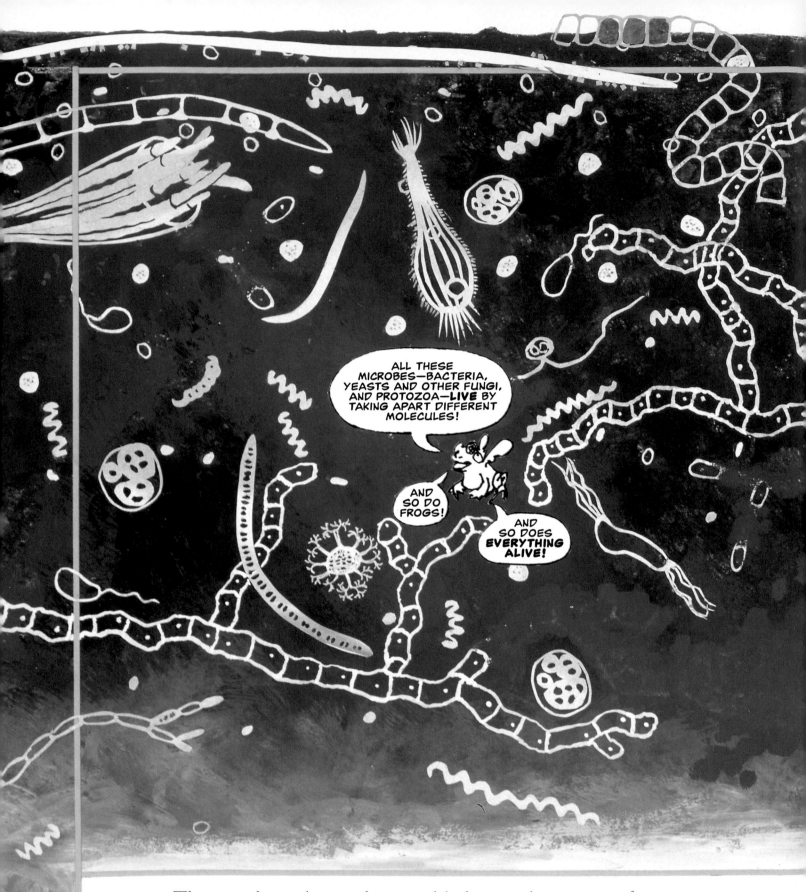

The man hoped microbes would change them into safe, tiny pieces. Waste in all sewage treatment facilities is broken down by microbes. But would these little life-forms be able to clean up thirty-three *poisons*?

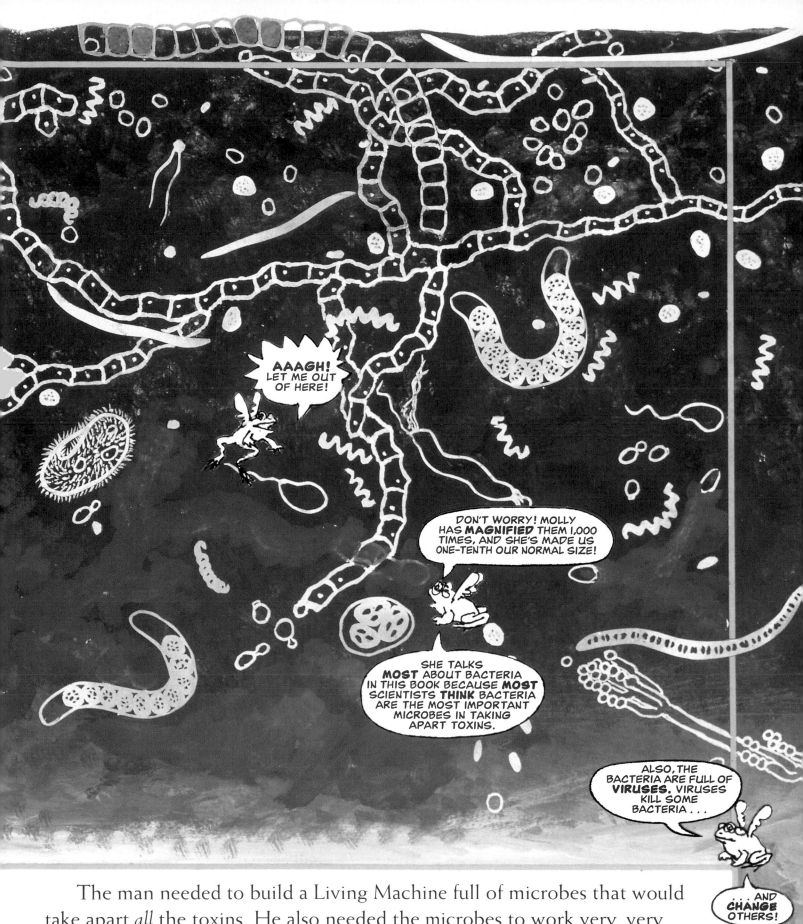

The man needed to build a Living Machine full of microbes that would take apart *all* the toxins. He also needed the microbes to work very, very fast, or the Living Machine would be too expensive to run.

The man thought, "Which microbes are the best at taking chemicals apart? Bacteria! If no bacteria existed, the world would be covered with the wastes and dead bodies of all the plants and animals that have ever lived."

In fact, bacteria make all life possible. Some bacteria pull chemicals out of the earth or the air and rearrange them into new chemicals that plants and animals need in order to live. And bacteria can take apart almost all substances, breaking big molecules into smaller ones. Some bacteria take apart meat, some take apart bones. And some bacteria take apart toxins, like those in the sludge from Chattanooga Creek.

The man flew home with the bottle of sludge. Right away he drove over to a salt marsh and dug up some mud. The mud was black and smelled like rotten eggs, which meant it was full of *anaerobic* bacteria—bacteria that are able to live without oxygen. Anaerobic bacteria take apart many of the worst toxins. But they work very, very slowly.

AND THE OCEAN TIDES FLUSH IT OUT TWICE A DAY!

BUT WE CAN'T LIVE HERE ANYWAY—IT'S SALT WATER!

He drove back with the marsh mud, poured it into a small tank outside his laboratory, and added to it:

- sixteen liters of water from a freshwater aquarium
- bits of rotten wood from an old railroad tie
- dead, moldy leaves from the woods
- bacteria he had bought from a bacteria company

The marsh mud, the rotten railroad tie, the moldy leaves, and the water from the aquarium were full of different kinds of bacteria and other microbes. He stirred them together as a sort of microbial soup, and he also added more food for the microbes—mostly a chemical called *acetate*.

The man hoped the microbes would take apart the toxins and change them into food for living things. In a Living Machine they would work much faster than in nature because they would be *warm, well fed,* and *concentrated,* and their *environment* inside the soup would *change* when it was stirred three times a day. But would they be able to take apart the toxins as well as their normal food?

The man poured three liters of Chattanooga Creek sludge, with all *its* bacteria, into the tank of microbial soup. He stirred, holding his breath so he wouldn't breathe the fumes. This sludge smelled truly *poisonous*. After he had stirred the muck all together, he turned on a little heater so the microbes would stay warm. He bubbled air up through the soup because most microbes are *aerobic*—they need oxygen to live. But he kept the soup very thick so there would always be places that air did not reach, where anaerobic bacteria could thrive.

Three times a day the man stirred his soup and added more food. Each time he stirred, the bacteria met new toxins and new environments.

With this "pulsed" mixing and changing of environments, many kinds of bacteria and other microbes were living in one tank, working together to take apart the toxins. Some kinds of bacteria could not survive in the sludge soup, and they died. Other kinds ate and breathed and multiplied. And bacteria multiply *very* fast. Under the best conditions, certain bacteria can divide every twenty minutes. So, in unlimited space, one bacterium could become 5,000,000,000,000,000,000,000,000 (five septillion) bacteria in a single *day*.

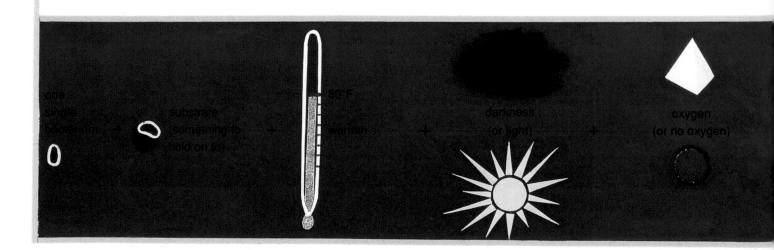

one single bacterium + substrate (something to hold on to) + 80°F warmth + darkness (or light) + oxygen (or no oxygen)

Every day the man also checked the second tank: a big cylindrical plastic aquarium from which he had gotten the water for the sludge tank. Inside, three kinds of fish were swimming around, green plants on the water's surface were bubbling out oxygen, snails on the tank walls were eating green algae and laying eggs, and one lone Louisiana Red crayfish was scratching through the mud on the round tank floor. A 300-watt lightbulb, always lit, hung next to the tank so the plants could always make oxygen, even at night. And bacteria were living wherever there was a surface they could hold on to.

This aquarium was the Bioassay Tank. The plants and animals inside were healthy now. When the man added water from the sludge tank, would they remain healthy, or would some get sick or even die? These plants and animals would be a "living test"—a bioassay—of how well the microbes in the sludge tank were breaking down the toxins into food.

Water Hyacinth

Salvinia

Elodea

Lymnaea

Ramshorn Snail

Armored Catfish

A **BIOASSAY** TESTS HOW A SUBSTANCE AFFECTS LIVING THINGS. IN THIS EXPERIMENT, IF AN ANIMAL DIES, THAT SHOWS THE SLUDGE IS PROBABLY TOO DANGEROUS FOR **HUMANS** AS WELL!

SO IF THESE ANIMALS DON'T DIE, MILLIONS OF OTHERS WON'T EITHER!

BUT ISN'T THERE A TEST THAT DOESN'T USE LIVING THINGS?

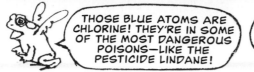

THOSE BLUE ATOMS ARE CHLORINE! THEY'RE IN SOME OF THE MOST DANGEROUS POISONS—LIKE THE PESTICIDE LINDANE!

CHLORINE IS ALSO **NECESSARY** TO ALL LIFE! BOTH THE COMBINATION AND THE AMOUNT MAKE THE DIFFERENCE!

NaCl
Sodium
Chloride
(table salt)

THE WAY ATOMS FIT TOGETHER MAKES A MOLECULE POISONOUS—OR NOT!

ALSO, A **FEW** MOLECULES OF A CHEMICAL MIGHT NOT HARM US—WHEN **MANY** WILL!

The reason bacteria can change these poisons into food is this: Microbes, the toxins in Chattanooga Creek, and all living things are made out of the same building blocks—the same chemical elements—*mostly*

Carbon   Hydrogen   Oxygen   Nitrogen

The difference between most poisons and most safe chemicals is *the way their elements are put together.* When poisons come apart, many of the pieces are safe food for plants, which use them to build stems and leaves. When animals eat plants, the elements from the plants get rearranged to build the animals' bodies.

The man knew that bacteria and other microbes would *eventually* take apart the poisons in the sludge. As the world has changed over millions of years and new molecules have formed in nature, new bacteria have always developed to take them apart. But the man didn't know if the microbes in his tank could take apart *all* the toxins or if they would work *fast* enough. The toxins were mostly made of molecules that were bound together very tightly. Most had been made by humans in the past 150 years. How much time would the microbes need to adapt to this new food?

Every day the man continued to stir the soup so that the different microbes would meet as many toxins as possible—and change, and eat, and multiply.

NH_3

Ammonia
molecule

CH_4

Methane
molecule

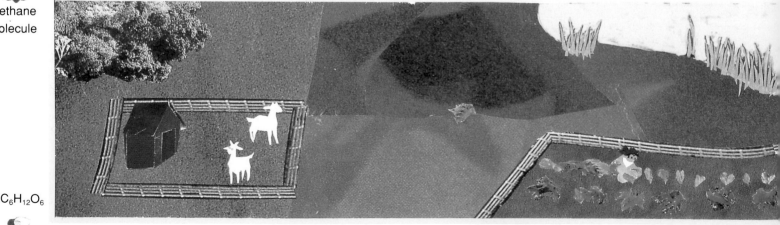

$C_6H_{12}O_6$

Glucose
(a sugar)

$C_{10}H_8$ Naphthalene
(mothballs)

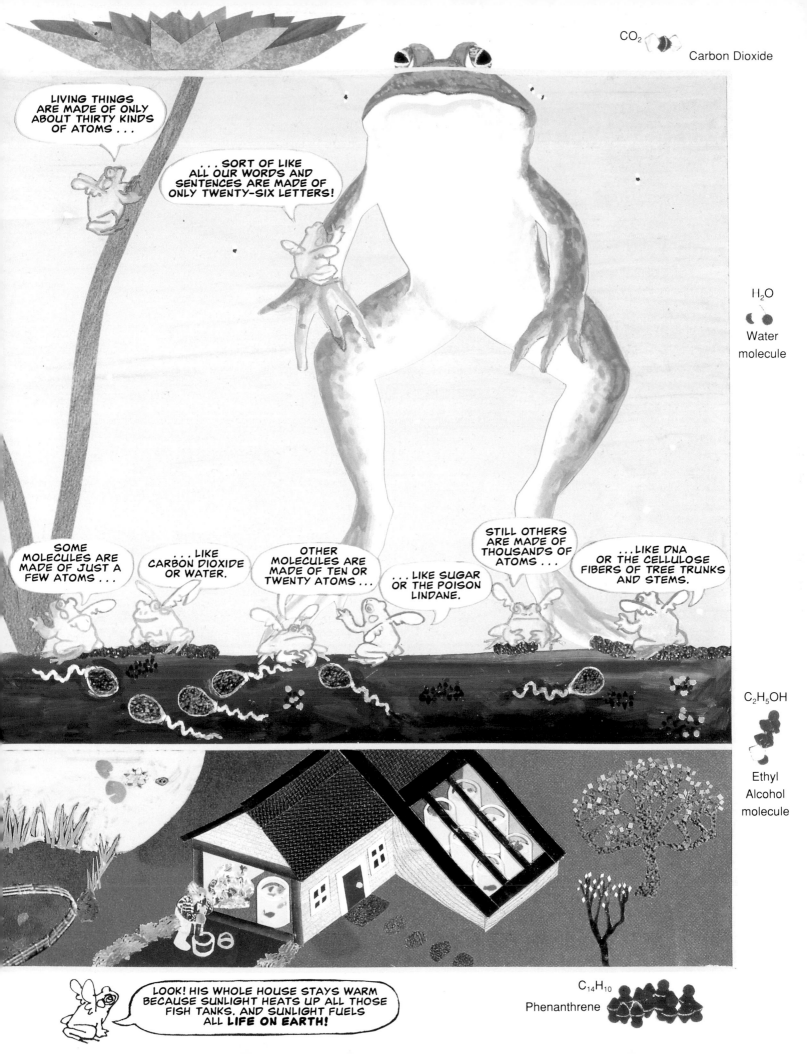

After five days the man saw *foam*. This foam was millions of tiny bubbles made by microbes hard at work. Microbes get energy by taking molecules apart (as all living creatures do), and they make gas as waste in the process (as we all do). They wouldn't be making bubbles if they weren't taking *something* apart, and they wouldn't be making so *many* bubbles if they weren't working very hard, and multiplying.

The man stirred the soup for eight long days, until it was foaming

all the way up to the lid. He was impatient to see if the water that had filtered to the top was clean yet. Also, he wanted the microbes from the two tanks to work together.

So he took a tiny amount of water from the Bioassay Tank and poured it into the foaming soup. He poured the same amount of water from on top of the soup into the Bioassay Tank. If there were toxins in the water seeping up from the sludge, the animals would let him know.

The next day, when the man returned, four of the fish were floating at the top of the tank, dead. He was worried. His system had to work quickly, or it would be too expensive to use for treating toxic waste. The dead fish showed that after eight days in the system even the *water* from the sludge was still *extremely* poisonous.

Yet the plants were still bubbling out oxygen, the snails were still laying eggs, and the Louisiana Red crayfish was still stirring everything around. The man opened the lid, took out the dead fish, and exchanged more water.

The next day all the fish were dead. They could not live with even a tiny amount of the toxins. The man took them out, thinking hard.

He had to make a decision: should he let the Living Machine rest for a couple of days, or should he continue to exchange water and risk killing the snails and crayfish?

Everything remaining in the tank seemed to be fine. So the man exchanged more liquids.

A LIVING MACHINE IS A MINIATURE MODEL OF THE REAL WORLD. IT HAS SUNLIGHT, WATER, WARMTH, LIVING THINGS, AND FOOD.

BACTERIA EAT **THEIR** FOOD, AND THE BREAKDOWN PRODUCTS GO TO FEED PLANTS.

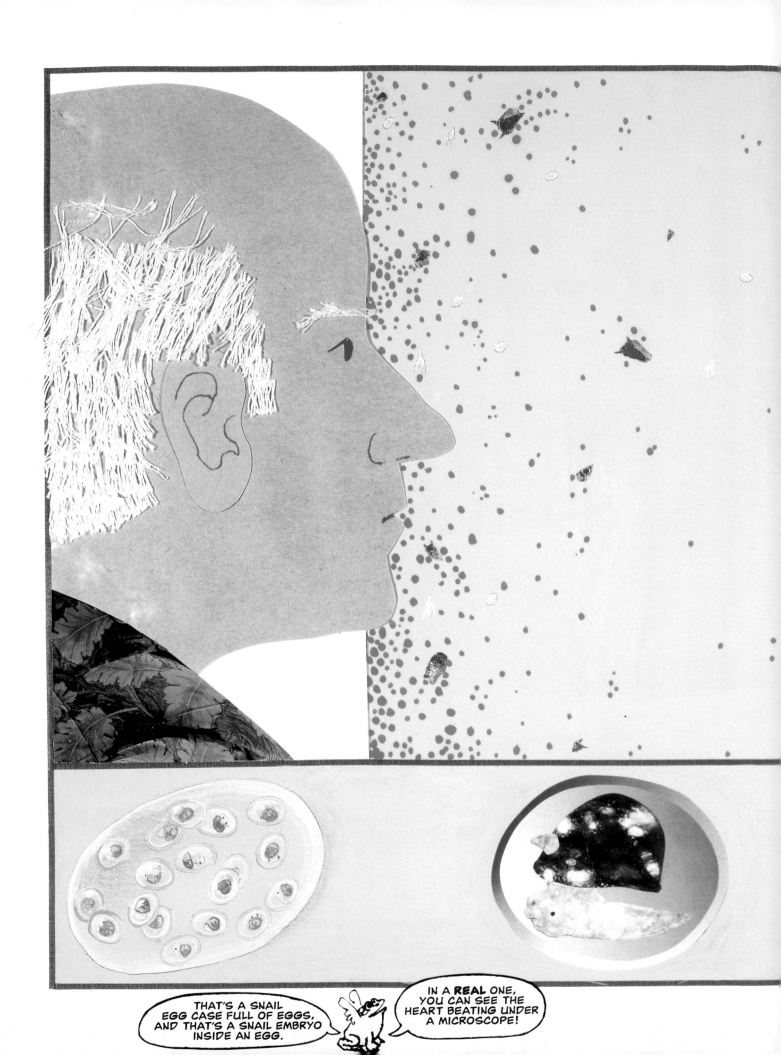

Every day he watched the tanks.

As he watched, he realized that the best measure of toxins in the system was the snails. If the snails stopped laying eggs, the man knew there were too many toxins, and he would stop exchanging water. In a day or so he would see that the snails were back to laying eggs. Only then would he exchange water again. As everything kept working, he gradually exchanged larger amounts of water, until he was up to two whole quarts a day.

After one month the man smelled no poisonous stench at all when he stirred the sludge tank. It was time to have a laboratory do a chemical analysis.

He filled two quart bottles with water from the Bioassay Tank. This water had run through the two tanks of the Living Machine for a whole month, with bacteria and other microbes in both tanks constantly taking apart whatever molecules they could. He hoped it would have very few toxins still floating in it. He sent the water to a government laboratory for scientists there to test.

THAT'S A PHOTO OF THE SURFACE OF A SNAIL'S **TONGUE!** IT LOOKS LIKE A CLOTH FULL OF SPIKES!

I SEE HOW SNAILS CAN SCRAPE UP SO MUCH ALGAE!

BUT HOW CAN SNAILS LIVE IN CONDITIONS THAT **DESTROY** OTHER ANIMALS?

ARE HUMANS TRYING TO FIND OUT?

He waited. He took long, solitary walks on the beach next to the salt marsh.

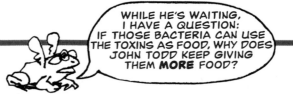

WHILE HE'S WAITING, I HAVE A QUESTION: IF THOSE BACTERIA CAN USE THE TOXINS AS FOOD, WHY DOES JOHN TODD KEEP GIVING THEM **MORE** FOOD?

In a month the report came back.

The tests showed that after thirty days in the Living Machine the water was essentially *pure!* The man was so happy he danced around the room and ran up and down the stairs. He called his friends on the telephone. "It works! It works! The water is clean!"

The Living Machine had passed its first test SPECTACULARLY!

It had now been two months since he had begun the experiment. It was time for the second, more important test: had the Living Machine cleaned the toxic sludge itself?

The man took the Living Machine apart. He took out samples of all the plants and animals, poured out five liters of water from the Bioassay Tank, and emptied out all of the foaming sludge soup. He packed everything up and sent it to the government laboratory, where scientists could measure the toxins remaining in each part of the system.

He waited.

At last he got back their report. Just like before, the water was clean. In addition, more than half the sludge in the three-liter sample from Chattanooga Creek was gone—broken down by microbes! From the whole system, twenty-one of the thirty-three toxins had decreased by more than half, and some had essentially disappeared—all in just two months! The man was thrilled! But then he read the last page of the report.

Three of the toxins were relatively unchanged and nine of them had increased! *Increased?* Why? How? The man looked and looked at the list of toxins. He couldn't understand what had happened. Was the idea of cleaning up Chattanooga Creek just a wild dream?

He called a chemist friend and described the situation. "Why are these toxins increasing?" he asked. "What can I do?"

The friend listened carefully, then said, "Your results *are* confusing. You'll have to repeat the experiment. But you *have* shown two things clearly.

"First, your bacteria are obviously thriving despite all the toxins, and they'll eventually break down many of them. Second, the behavior of your snails seems to show that the Living Machine *is* working. Keep the system going a bit longer and add some fish again to see how they do."

DIFFERENT KINDS OF BACTERIA TAKE APART DIFFERENT PARTS OF TOXINS.

AND WE NEED **ALL** OF THEM WORKING **TOGETHER** TO TAKE THE TOXINS APART **COMPLETELY.**

But the man couldn't keep it going any longer. He had taken it apart.
It didn't exist anymore.

He looked sadly at the summer trees. If only he could get the machine
to work *faster,* so *more* bacteria could meet *more* toxins, and multiply. . . .

Suddenly he jumped up. "I know how to do it!" he yelled.

He began to plan a new, faster Living Machine for Chattanooga Creek.

BUT IT LOOKS
LIKE A **MESS** TO HUMANS.
THEY DON'T UNDERSTAND
MUCH ABOUT HOW IT
ALL **WORKS!**

THAT'S OK.
THE BACTERIA
CAN TEACH THEM
—IF THE HUMANS
WILL JUST PAY
ATTENTION!

To the aquarium, he added an inner tank full of pumice stones, which float in water, and he bubbled air into them.

IF I MANAGED THE MACHINE, I'D RUN THE PUMPS IN A **RHYTHM!** NATURE ALWAYS USES RHYTHM!

I HEARD **METALS** ARE **POISONS.** IF METALS ARE IN THE SLUDGE, HOW WILL JOHN TODD GET RID OF THEM?

Most microbes need something to hang on to in order to live, and so far the best microbial "nest" in his tank had been the plant roots. With the addition of the pumice stones, there would be thousands of times more surface area, where billions and billions more microbes could live—and where they could multiply into googols more, all taking apart toxins.

SOME **HEAVY** METALS ARE POISONOUS, BUT ALL LIVING THINGS **NEED** TINY AMOUNTS OF MANY METALS TO **LIVE**. (BUT WE DON'T NEED **ANY** LEAD OR MERCURY.) HIGHER DOSES CAN BE POISONOUS. THERE **ARE** SOME HEAVY METALS IN THE SLUDGE FROM CHATTANOOGA CREEK, BECAUSE THEY WERE USED IN SOME FACTORIES.

SOME **BACTERIA** AND SOME **MOSSES** ATTRACT METALS. JOHN TODD WILL PROBABLY RUN THE SLUDGE THROUGH SIDE STATIONS FILLED WITH THESE BACTERIA AND MOSSES TO PULL OUT THE METALS. THEN HE WILL HARVEST THE BACTERIA AND MOSS. WHEN HE GETS ENOUGH, HE WILL **BURN** OR **MELT** THEM, TAKE THE METALS FROM THE **ASHES** AND **REUSE** THEM!

This is the end of the story so far—of one man who tried to see if a tiny bit of toxic sludge could be cleaned by a very small Living Machine. The results of the experiment weren't perfect, but they were very, very good. The next step would be to build a big Living Machine next to the creek to see how well a large amount of toxic sludge can be cleaned.

The most important step in cleaning up toxic waste is to make

LIFE IS LIKE AN INTRICATE, ENDLESS DANCE.

FACTORIES MAKE THINGS THAT HUMANS NEED OR WANT, BUT SOME FACTORY WASTES ARE POISONOUS.